231 two hundred and thirty-one

Write how many in figures and words.

How many?

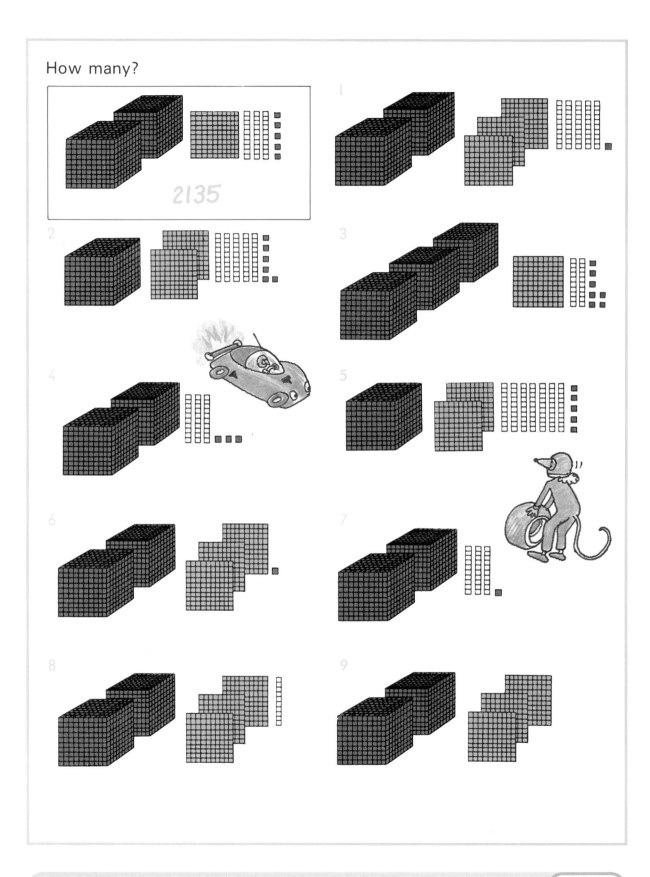

2135

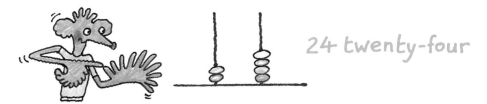

24 twenty-four

Write how many in figures and words.

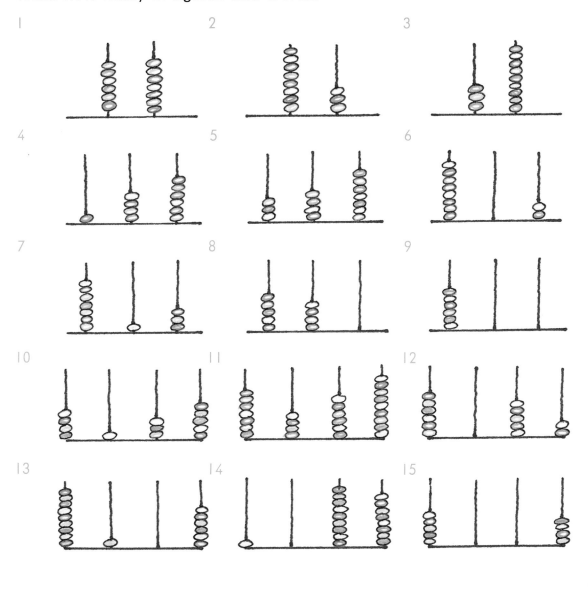

Copy and complete by writing < or > instead of the ●

1	237 ● 156	2	759 ● 781	3	683 ● 686

1   237 ● 156   2   759 ● 781   3   683 ● 686

4   945 ● 946   5   605 ● 650   6   382 ● 390

7   184 ● 799   8   593 ● 589   9   1796 ● 1787

10   5948 ● 5938   11   8321 ● 8320   12   4036 ● 4035

13   1036 ● 974   14   953 ● 2065   15   7402 ● 5967

16   1000 ● 990   17   999 ● 1000   18   3421 ● 3457

19   6217 ● 6271   20   6308 ● 6301   21   6635 ● 6636

22   7630 ● 7603   23   5936 ● 5928   24   1000 ● 1999

Copy and complete:

1	2	3	4	5	6	7	8
4	5	3	4	9	4	6	1
3	4	5	3	1	2	2	8
+6	+5	+7	+7	+8	+6	+8	+9

9	10	11	12	13	14	15	16
3	1	2	7	5	8	6	5
4	7	9	1	5	2	4	1
2	4	4	3	3	5	2	4
+5	+5	+4	+2	+2	+3	+4	+7

17	18	19	20	21	22	23	24
5	3	6	4	3	5	7	5
3	3	9	7	3	1	4	6
8	6	1	2	2	4	1	0
+2	+4	+3	+4	+5	+1	+2	+5

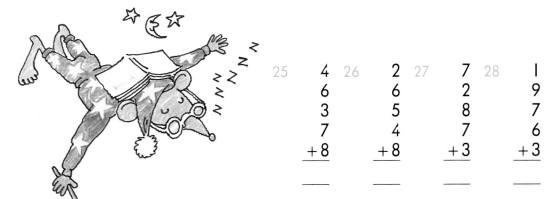

25	26	27	28
4	2	7	1
6	6	2	9
3	5	8	7
7	4	7	6
+8	+8	+3	+3

```
 38        8 + 9 = 17. The 17 units are regrouped
+29                  as 1 ten and 7 units.
 67
  1
```

Copy and complete:

1 25
   +36
	2 74
	   +17
		3 57
		   +29
			4 83
			   + 9
				5 35
				   +28

6 36
   +47
	7 8
	   +42
		8 51
		   +29
			9 57
			   +33
				10 32
				   +19

```
 4 1
 5 1         The 51 is regrouped as 40 + 11
-28
 23
```

11 42
   −24
	12 27
	   −19
		13 50
		   −21
			14 63
			   −17
				15 94
				   −38

16 81
   −59
	17 75
	   −27
		18 46
		   −38
			19 78
			   −19
				20 90
				   −33

21 Add 37 to 45.   22 Take 19 from 70.
23 Find (a) the sum of, and (b) the difference between 43 and 28.

1　Jessica weighs 56 kg. Ben weighs 70 kg.
How much heavier is Ben than Jessica? ＿＿＿ kg

2　Ben walked 37 kilometres.
Jessica walked 19 kilometres more than Ben.
How far did Jessica walk? ＿＿＿ kilometres

3　Ben has £25. Jessica has £18.
(a) How much do they have altogether? ＿＿＿
(b) How much more has Ben got than Jessica? ＿＿＿

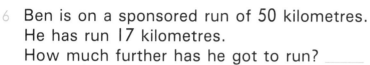

4　Jessica saved £13.
Ben saved £9 less than Jessica.
How much did Ben save? ＿＿＿

5　Jessica was given £50 at Chrismas.
She bought a dress for £16 and some shoes for £27.
(a) How much did Jessica spend? ＿＿＿
(b) How much did she have left? ＿＿＿

6　Ben is on a sponsored run of 50 kilometres.
He has run 17 kilometres.
How much further has he got to run? ＿＿＿

Give each missing number.

$4 + \underline{5} = 9$

1	$3 + \underline{} = 10$	2	$2 + \underline{} = 11$	3	$4 + \underline{} = 10$
4	$4 + \underline{} = 12$	5	$5 + \underline{} = 14$	6	$5 + \underline{} = 12$
7	$5 + \underline{} = 11$	8	$8 + \underline{} = 13$	9	$8 + \underline{} = 14$
10	$7 + \underline{} = 13$	11	$7 + \underline{} = 15$	12	$7 + \underline{} = 10$
13	$8 + \underline{} = 11$	14	$9 + \underline{} = 13$	15	$8 + \underline{} = 17$
16	$9 + \underline{} = 15$	17	$3 + \underline{} = 12$	18	$2 + \underline{} = 10$
19	$\underline{} + 4 = 11$	20	$\underline{} + 8 = 12$	21	$\underline{} + 5 = 13$
22	$\underline{} + 7 = 12$	23	$\underline{} + 6 = 15$	24	$\underline{} + 6 = 14$
25	$\underline{} + 9 = 14$	26	$\underline{} + 7 = 11$	27	$\underline{} + 9 = 12$
28	$\underline{} + 6 = 11$	29	$\underline{} + 9 = 17$	30	$\underline{} + 7 = 14$
31	$\underline{} + 8 = 16$	32	$\underline{} + 8 = 15$	33	$\underline{} + 6 = 12$
34	$\underline{} + 4 = 13$	35	$\underline{} + 6 = 13$	36	$\underline{} + 9 = 18$

Add across. Add down.

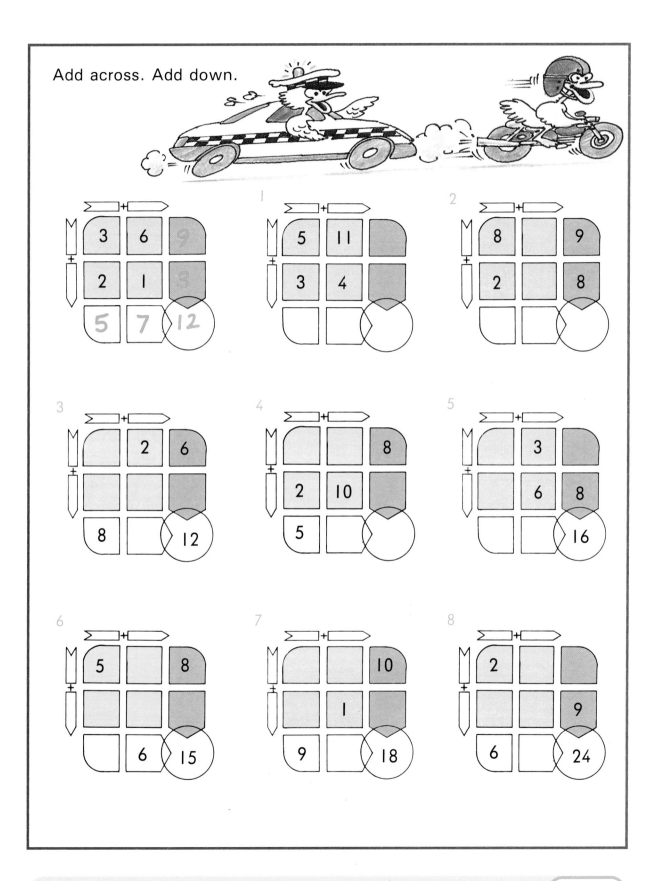

| 29p | 80p | 38p | 54p |

1 Which is the total cost of:

(a) the sugar and the jam? _____

(b) the cereal and the tea? _____

(c) the tea and the sugar? _____

2 Find the difference in the cost of:

(a) the sugar and the cereal. _____

(b) the tea and the jam. _____

(c) the jam and the sugar. _____

3 Carol had 91p. How much would she have left if she bought:

(a) the sugar _____   (b) the jam _____

(c) the cereal _____   (d) the tea _____?

Subtract,

$$\begin{array}{r} ^2\!\!\not{3}^1 \\ -17 \\ \hline 14 \end{array}$$

Check by adding,

$$\begin{array}{r} 14 \\ +17 \\ \hline 31 \\ \scriptstyle 1 \end{array}$$

Check each subtraction by adding.

1. $\begin{array}{r} 43 \\ -18 \\ \hline \end{array}$
2. $\begin{array}{r} 53 \\ -29 \\ \hline \end{array}$
3. $\begin{array}{r} 45 \\ -26 \\ \hline \end{array}$
4. $\begin{array}{r} 31 \\ -19 \\ \hline \end{array}$
5. $\begin{array}{r} 32 \\ -8 \\ \hline \end{array}$

6. $\begin{array}{r} 62 \\ -45 \\ \hline \end{array}$
7. $\begin{array}{r} 71 \\ -36 \\ \hline \end{array}$
8. $\begin{array}{r} 42 \\ -35 \\ \hline \end{array}$
9. $\begin{array}{r} 51 \\ -26 \\ \hline \end{array}$
10. $\begin{array}{r} 85 \\ -49 \\ \hline \end{array}$

11. $\begin{array}{r} 82 \\ -75 \\ \hline \end{array}$
12. $\begin{array}{r} 93 \\ -46 \\ \hline \end{array}$
13. $\begin{array}{r} 88 \\ -49 \\ \hline \end{array}$
14. $\begin{array}{r} 67 \\ -48 \\ \hline \end{array}$
15. $\begin{array}{r} 75 \\ -28 \\ \hline \end{array}$

16. $\begin{array}{r} 437 \\ -156 \\ \hline \end{array}$
17. $\begin{array}{r} 321 \\ -181 \\ \hline \end{array}$
18. $\begin{array}{r} 246 \\ -194 \\ \hline \end{array}$
19. $\begin{array}{r} 603 \\ -473 \\ \hline \end{array}$

20. $\begin{array}{r} 587 \\ -193 \\ \hline \end{array}$
21. $\begin{array}{r} 626 \\ -383 \\ \hline \end{array}$
22. $\begin{array}{r} 319 \\ -54 \\ \hline \end{array}$
23. $\begin{array}{r} 426 \\ -374 \\ \hline \end{array}$

One pound = 100 pence.
£1 = 100p

One pound and twenty-three pence is written as £1.23.
£1.23 = 100p + 23p = 123p.
178p = 100p + 78p = £1 + 78p = £1.78.

How many pence?

1 £1.10 _____   2 £1.68 _____   3 £2.95 _____

4 £1.07 _____   5 £2.40 _____   6 £3.92 _____

7 £5.32 _____   8 £6.01 _____   9 £9.00 _____

Copy and complete:

10 142p = 100p + 42p = £_____   11 216p = 200p + _____p = £_____

12 189p = _____ + _____ = _____   13 275p = _____ + _____ = _____

14 104p = _____ + _____ = _____   15 206p = _____ + _____ = _____

31p is written as £0.31 (read as: nought point three one pounds)

16 Write in pounds:

(a) 57p _____   (b) 19p _____   (c) 7p _____

17 Write in pence:

(a) £0.48 _____   (b) £0.92 _____   (c) £0.03 _____

Copy and complete the multiplications.

1 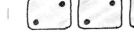 $2 \times \underline{\hspace{2cm}} = \underline{\hspace{2cm}}$

2 $3 \times \underline{\hspace{2cm}} = \underline{\hspace{1cm}}$

3 $4 \times \underline{\hspace{2cm}} = \underline{\hspace{2cm}}$

4  $\underline{\hspace{1.5cm}} \times \underline{\hspace{1.5cm}} = \underline{\hspace{1cm}}$

5

$\underline{\hspace{2cm}} \times \underline{\hspace{2cm}} = \underline{\hspace{2cm}}$

6 (a)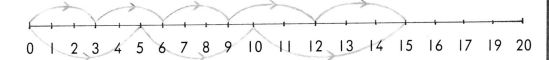

$3 \times 5 = \underline{\hspace{1.5cm}}$ $5 \times 3 = \underline{\hspace{1.5cm}}$ so $3 \times 5 = \underline{\hspace{1.5cm}} \times \underline{\hspace{1.5cm}}$

(b) $2 \times 3 = \underline{\hspace{1.5cm}}$ $3 \times 2 = \underline{\hspace{1.5cm}}$ so $2 \times 3 = \underline{\hspace{1.5cm}} \times \underline{\hspace{1.5cm}}$

(c) $4 \times 5 = \underline{\hspace{1.5cm}}$ $5 \times 4 = \underline{\hspace{1.5cm}}$ so $\underline{\hspace{1.5cm}} \times \underline{\hspace{1.5cm}} = \underline{\hspace{1.5cm}} \times \underline{\hspace{1.5cm}}$

(d) $2 \times 10 = \underline{\hspace{1.5cm}}$ $10 \times 2 = \underline{\hspace{1.5cm}}$ so $\underline{\hspace{1.5cm}} \times \underline{\hspace{1.5cm}} = \underline{\hspace{1.5cm}} \times \underline{\hspace{1.5cm}}$

7 Write as a multiplication and give the answer.

(a) $4 + 4 + 4 + 4 + 4 = \underline{\hspace{1.5cm}} \times \underline{\hspace{1.5cm}} = \underline{\hspace{1.5cm}}$

(b) $10 + 10 + 10 + 10 + 10 = \underline{\hspace{1.5cm}} \times \underline{\hspace{1.5cm}} = \underline{\hspace{1.5cm}}$

(c) $5 + 5 + 5 + 5 + 5 + 5 = \underline{\hspace{1.5cm}} \times \underline{\hspace{1.5cm}} = \underline{\hspace{1.5cm}}$

$$4 \times 2 = 8 \qquad 3 \times 1 = 3 \qquad 2 \times 0 = 0$$

Copy and complete.

1   $3 \times 2 = \underline{}$ 2 $5 \times 2 = \underline{}$ 3 $5 \times 0 = \underline{}$

4   $8 \times 1 = \underline{}$ 5 $8 \times 2 = \underline{}$ 6 $2 \times 2 = \underline{}$

7   $4 \times 1 = \underline{}$ 8 $5 \times 1 = \underline{}$ 9 $2 \times 1 = \underline{}$

10   $8 \times 0 = \underline{}$ 11 $4 \times 0 = \underline{}$ 12 $9 \times 1 = \underline{}$

13   $4 \times 3 = \underline{}$ 14 $9 \times 2 = \underline{}$ 15 $7 \times 0 = \underline{}$

16   $3 \times 3 = \underline{}$ 17 $6 \times 1 = \underline{}$ 18 $1 \times 0 = \underline{}$

19   $7 \times 4 = \underline{}$ 20 $1 \times 4 = \underline{}$ 21 $1 \times 2 = \underline{}$

22   $1 \times 3 = \underline{}$ 23 $8 \times 3 = \underline{}$ 24 $7 \times 1 = \underline{}$

25   $6 \times 0 = \underline{}$ 26 $1 \times 5 = \underline{}$ 27 $5 \times 3 = \underline{}$

28   $6 \times 2 = \underline{}$ 29 $9 \times 4 = \underline{}$ 30 $6 \times 5 = \underline{}$

Multiply. Then decode to answer the riddle:
Which travels faster – heat or cold?

1 $2 \times 5 =$ ___ 10 | H

2 $8 \times 2 =$ ___ | ___

3 $6 \times 0 =$ ___ | ___

4 $5 \times 3 =$ ___ | ___

12 $1 \times 1 =$ ___ | ___

13 $2 \times 4 =$ ___ | ___

14 $9 \times 1 =$ ___ | ___

23 $5 \times 0 =$ ___ | ___

24 $6 \times 2 =$ ___ | ___

25 $8 \times 1 =$ ___ | ___

26 $2 \times 2 =$ ___ | ___

27 $3 \times 2 =$ ___ | ___

5 $7 \times 1 =$ ___ | ___

6 $4 \times 4 =$ ___ | ___

7 $3 \times 4 =$ ___ | ___

8 $8 \times 0 =$ ___ | ___

9 $3 \times 3 =$ ___ | ___

10 $7 \times 2 =$ ___ | ___

11 $8 \times 2 =$ ___ | ___

15 $6 \times 2 =$ ___ | ___

16 $9 \times 0 =$ ___ | ___

17 $2 \times 1 =$ ___ | ___

18 $4 \times 3 =$ ___ | ___

19 $7 \times 0 =$ ___ | ___

20 $3 \times 5 =$ ___ | ___

21 $6 \times 2 =$ ___ | ___

22 $5 \times 2 =$ ___ | ___

0	1	2	4	6	7	8	9	10	12	14	15	16
A	Y	N	L	D	B	O	U	H	C	S	T	E

Solve.

1   9

     3

How many puppies altogether?

2   9

     3

How many more spotted puppies?

3   8

     2

How many more white cats?

4   8

     2

How many cats altogether?

5   17

     14

How many rabbits altogether?

6   17

     14

How many more white rabbits?

7   12 puppies in a box.

    5 jumped out.

    How many were left?

8   19 fish in one tank.

    8 fish in another.

    How many fish altogether?

9   21 birds in a cage.
    13 could talk.
    How many could not talk?

10   24 large tortoises in one box.
    8 small tortoises in another.
    How many altogether?

Here are some more problems.

There were 14 boys and 11 girls on a school bus.
How many children altogether?
Write an equation, then solve it.

14 + 11 = ___   14 + 11 = 25
There were 25 children on the bus.

Solve these problems in the same way.

1 12 children were playing.
   7 had to go home.
   How many were left?

2 John had 18p.
   His mother gave him 16p.
   How much did he then have?

3 Ruth spent 30p.
   She had 25p left.
   How much did she have to start
   with?

4 14 girls were playing.
   15 boys joined them.
   How many children were
   playing altogether?

5 One box holds 4 cakes.
   Rob bought 3 boxes.
   How many cakes did he have?

6 One box holds 10 marbles.
   How many marbles will there
   be in 5 boxes?

7 Angie had 20 sweets.
   She ate 13 of them.
   How many did she have left?

8 Stephen had 18 ducks and 26
   chickens. How many birds did
   he have altogether?

Karen and Carol share 8 apples equally.
How many apples will they each get?

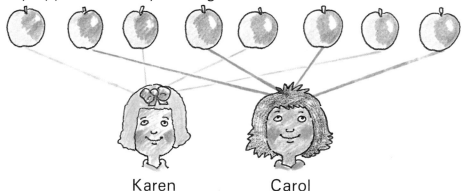

Karen   Carol

$8 \div 2 = 4$. They get 4 apples each.

($8 \div 2 = 4$ means 'eight divided by two equals four.')

Do these divisions.

1 Alan, Ben and Colin share
   6 comics equally.
   How many comics will each boy
   get? _____

Alan   Ben   Colin

2 Karen and Carol share
   8p equally:
   How much will they get each? _____

3 Alan, Ben and Colin share
   12 sweets equally.
   How many sweets will they get each? _____

4 Carol, Ben and Colin share 12 stamps equally.
   How many stamps will they get each? _____

Copy and complete. $25 \div 5 = 5$

1   $8 \div 2 =$ ___   2 $12 \div 3 =$ ___   3 $2 \div 2 =$ ___

4   $6 \div 2 =$ ___   5 $6 \div 3 =$ ___   6 $10 \div 2 =$ ___

7   $9 \div 3 =$ ___   8 $15 \div 3 =$ ___   9 $4 \div 2 =$ ___

10   $16 \div 2 =$ ___   11 $4 \div 4 =$ ___   12 $27 \div 3 =$ ___

13   $18 \div 3 =$ ___   14 $20 \div 2 =$ ___

15   $24 \div 3 =$ ___   16 $12 \div 2 =$ ___

17   $10 \div 5 =$ ___   18 $8 \div 4 =$ ___

19   $14 \div 2 =$ ___   20 $20 \div 5 =$ ___

21   $16 \div 4 =$ ___   22 $5 \div 5 =$ ___

23   $3 \div 3 =$ ___   24 $24 \div 4 =$ ___

25   $18 \div 2 =$ ___   26 $12 \div 4 =$ ___

27   $21 \div 3 =$ ___

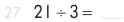

Write the answers:

1 10 🥚

   2 🥚 in each 🌻

   How many 🌻 ? _____

2 15 🦴

   3 🦴 for each 🐕

   How many 🐕 ? _____

3 16 🇺

   4 🇺 on each. 🐴

   How many 🐴 ? _____

4 30 🥔

   5 🥔 in each 🛍

   How many 🛍 ? _____

5 20 📮

   4 📮 for each ✉

   How many ✉ ? _____

6 20 🎀

   2 🎀 on each 👧

   How many 👧 ? _____

7 50 ✏

   10 ✏ in each 📦

   How many 📦 ? _____

8 15 ☝

   5 ☝ on each 🖐

   How many 🖐 ? _____

9 18 🎲

   3 🎲 in each ☕

   How many ☕ ? _____

10 30 🦶

    10 🦶 on each 👦

    How many 👦 ? _____

Copy and complete. $4 \times 4 = \underline{16}$

1   $4 \times 3 = \underline{}$ 2 $9 \times 1 = \underline{}$ 3 $8 \times 4 = \underline{}$

4   $9 \times 2 = \underline{}$ 5 $1 \times 1 = \underline{}$ 6 $3 \times 5 = \underline{}$

7   $8 \times 5 = \underline{}$ 8 $2 \times 4 = \underline{}$ 9 $5 \times 0 = \underline{}$

10   $7 \times 1 = \underline{}$ 11 $9 \times 5 = \underline{}$ 12 $4 \times 5 = \underline{}$

13   $5 \times 4 = \underline{}$ 14 $7 \times 2 = \underline{}$ 15 $6 \times 4 = \underline{}$

16   $9 \times 3 = \underline{}$ 17 $6 \times 1 = \underline{}$ 18 $7 \times 3 = \underline{}$

19   $6 \times 3 = \underline{}$ 20 $7 \times 5 = \underline{}$ 21 $5 \times 5 = \underline{}$

22   $12 \div 2 = \underline{}$ 23 $4 \div 2 = \underline{}$ 24 $9 \div 3 = \underline{}$

25   $4 \div 1 = \underline{}$ 26 $12 \div 4 = \underline{}$ 27 $20 \div 5 = \underline{}$

28   $10 \div 2 = \underline{}$ 29 $15 \div 3 = \underline{}$ 30 $16 \div 4 = \underline{}$

31   $0 \div 4 = \underline{}$ 32 $28 \div 4 = \underline{}$ 33 $5 \div 1 = \underline{}$

34   $6 \div 2 = \underline{}$ 35 $10 \div 5 = \underline{}$ 36 $30 \div 5 = \underline{}$

37   $24 \div 4 = \underline{}$ 38 $24 \div 3 = \underline{}$ 39 $15 \div 5 = \underline{}$

Brackets tell us what to do first.

$(10 - 2) \times 3 = 8 \times 3 = 24$

$8 - (2 \times 4) = 8 - 8 = 0$

Copy and complete.

1   $7 + (9 - 4) = 7 + \underline{\quad} = \underline{\quad}$ 2 $(9 - 3) - 1 = \underline{\quad} - 1 = \underline{\quad}$

3   $(4 + 3) \times 2 = \underline{\quad} \times 2 = \underline{\quad}$ 4 $4 + (3 \times 2) = 4 + \underline{\quad} = \underline{\quad}$

5   $(6 \div 2) + 1 = \underline{\quad} + 1 = \underline{\quad}$ 6 $6 \div (2 + 1) = 6 \div \underline{\quad} = \underline{\quad}$

7   $(30 \div 3) + 2 = \underline{\quad} + 2 = \underline{\quad}$ 8 $30 \div (3 + 2) = 30 \div \underline{\quad} = \underline{\quad}$

9   Tariq bought 3 sweets costing 4p each
and 5 sweets costing 2p each.
Complete to find how much Tariq spent.

$(3 \times \underline{\quad})p + (5 \times \underline{\quad})p = \underline{\quad}p + \underline{\quad}p = \underline{\quad}p.$

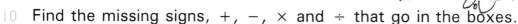

10   Find the missing signs, $+$, $-$, $\times$ and $\div$ that go in the boxes.
    (a) $(4 \boxed{} 2) \boxed{} 6 = 14$ (b) $(10 \boxed{} 2) \boxed{} 4 = 1$
    (c) $7 \boxed{} (5 \boxed{} 2) = 17$ (d) $2 \boxed{} (3 \boxed{} 4) = 24.$

Copy and complete each division table.

÷ 2

6	3
0	
8	
10	
14	
4	
2	
12	
16	
18	

÷ 3

9	3
21	
15	
3	
24	
6	
27	
0	
18	
12	

÷ 4

16	4
8	
4	
32	
12	
28	
24	
36	
20	
0	

÷ 5

45	9
0	
10	
15	
20	
30	
40	
35	
5	
25	

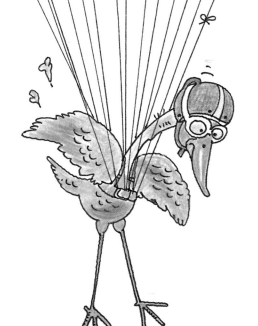

Solve.

1. Yesterday, Mr Nahar checked the tyres on 5 aeroplanes. Each aeroplane had 6 tyres. How many tyres did he check altogether?

2. Mr Nahar also checked 18 jet engines. If each aeroplane had 3 jet engines, how many aeroplanes did he check?

3. There are 5 members of the Williams family. If each passenger is allowed 3 pieces of luggage, how much luggage are they allowed?

4. A family of 4 had 20 pieces of luggage. They each had the same number of pieces. How many did they each have?

5. There are 4 flights to Edinburgh each day. How many flights are there in a week?

6. There are 25 flights to Paris from Monday to Friday. How many flights to Paris are there each weekday?

Round to the nearest ten.

1

← 40 41 42 43 44 45 46 47 48 49 50 →

41

2

← 10 11 12 13 14 15 16 17 18 19 20 →

18

3 48
7 52

4 45
8 162

5 11
9 115

6 15
10 279

Round to the nearest hundred.

11

← 300 310 320 330 340 350 360 370 380 390 400 →

327

12

← 400 410 420 430 440 450 460 470 480 490 500 →

481

13 354

14 350

15 520

16 549

17 614

18 250

19 149

20 863

We can round numbers in different ways.

4378 people live in Bagsville.

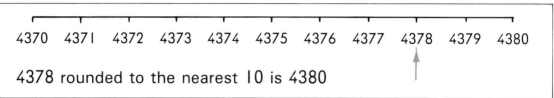

4370 4371 4372 4373 4374 4375 4376 4377 4378 4379 4380

4378 rounded to the nearest 10 is 4380

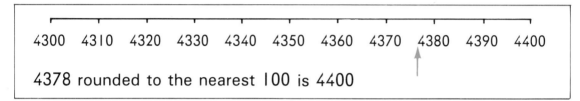

4300 4310 4320 4330 4340 4350 4360 4370 4380 4390 4400

4378 rounded to the nearest 100 is 4400

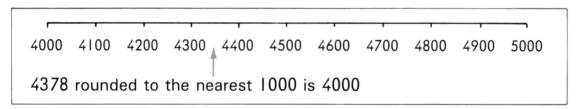

4000 4100 4200 4300 4400 4500 4600 4700 4800 4900 5000

4378 rounded to the nearest 1000 is 4000

Copy this table.

Round the population numbers for these villages and small towns.

Village or small town*	Number living there	Round to the nearest 10	Round to the nearest 100	Round to the nearest 1000
1	3925			
2	5478			
3	2837			
4	4766			
5	3214			
6	7084			
7	6198			
8	2239			

* invent your own names if you like.

Here are some Roman numbers:

I is I	V is 5	X is 10

I	II	III	IV	V	VI	VII	VIII	IX	X
1	2	3	4	5	6	7	8	9	10

When the smaller number is on the left it is **subtracted**.

IX means I is subtracted from 10 giving 9, so IX = 9.

If the smaller number (or numbers) is on the right it is **added**.

VII means 5 + 1 + 1 or 7.

XX means 10 + 10 and IV is 5 − 1

So XXIV means 24.

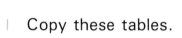

1 Copy these tables.

Complete the Roman numbers from 10 up to 30.

X	XI									
10	11	12	13	14	15	16	17	18	19	20

XXI								XXIX	
21	22	23	24	25	26	27	28	29	30

2 Write our numbers for

(a) XXXI _____   (b) XXXV _____   (c) XIX _____

3 Write the Roman numbers for

(a) 17 _____   (b) 33 _____   (c) 18 _____

4 Write today's date as a Roman number _____

Step 1

Add units, regroup.

```
  58
+ 29
————
   7
   1
```

Step 2

Add tens.

```
  58
+ 29
————
  87
   1
```

Copy and complete.

Round the numbers to the nearest 10 and estimate first.

1   27   2   36   3   42   4   75   5   23
    + 35   + 49   + 28   + 18   + 59

6   45   7   68   8   54   9   67   10   75
    + 37   + 27   + 39   + 26   + 18

11   75   12   87   13   61   14   76   15   83
    − 18   − 65   − 5   − 59   − 9

16   70   17   91   18   64
    − 53   − 65   − 45

19   32   20   86   21   53
    + 87   − 72   + 73

How much money?

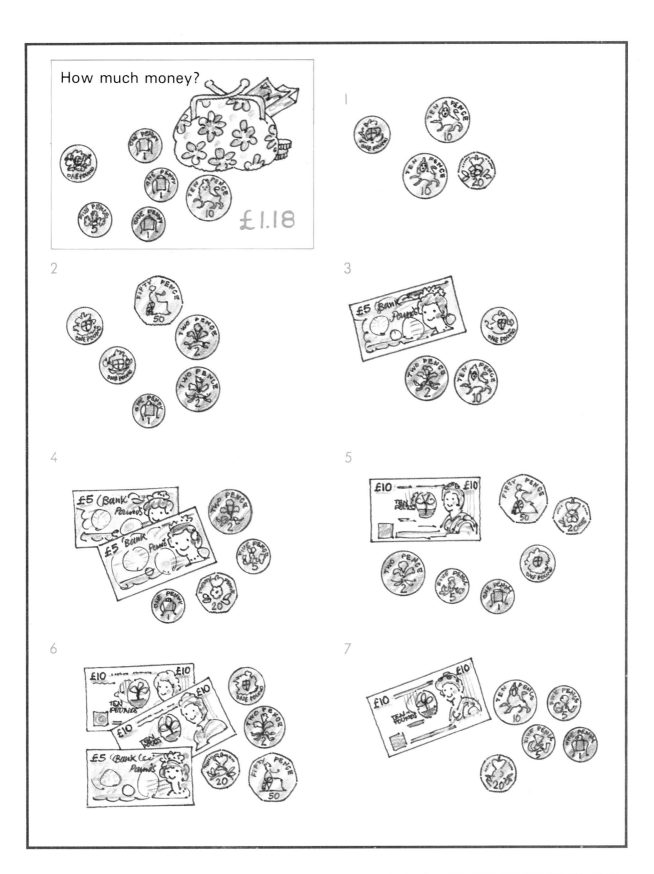

£1.18

£1.19　　　　£2.15　　　　£1.46

£2.49　　　　£1.95　　　　£2.27

Solve.

1　What is the total price of

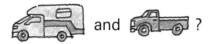 and ?

2　What is the total price of

and ?

3　You buy a

and a

What is the total cost?

4　You buy a

and a

What is the total cost?

5　If you buy a  and a

, how much do they

cost altogether?

6　How much would 2

cost?

7　If you bought the

the , how much

money would you need?

8　If you bought the and

the , how much

money would you need?

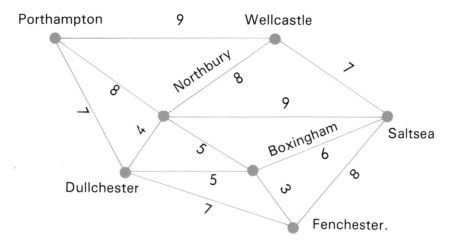

The distances on the map are all in kilometres.

Find these distances.

1   From Porthampton to Wellcastle and then to Saltsea.

2   From Northbury to Boxingham and then to Fenchester.

3   From Porthampton to Dullchester, then to Fenchester and then to Saltsea.

4   From Northbury to Boxingham, then to Saltsea and then to Wellcastle.

5   Which is the longer distance and how much longer is it?
    (a)   From Porthampton to Northbury or from Boxingham to Dullchester?
    (b)   From Northbury to Wellcastle or from Fenchester to Dullchester?

6   Which is the shortest route:
    (a)   From Porthampton to Boxingham?
    (b)   From Porthampton to Saltsea?
    (c)   From Porthampton to Fenchester?

```
   16
   35
 + 21
   72
```

Copy and complete.

1	2	3	4	5
36	16	8	71	28
28	48	15	30	6
+ 49	+ 74	+ 96	+ 59	+ 57

6	7	8	9	10
15	5	8	13	55
87	39	45	72	86
+ 62	+ 74	+ 89	+ 94	+ 90

11	12	13	14	15
6	52	67	60	82
92	86	46	38	43
+ 87	+ 15	+ 49	+ 74	+ 76

16	17	18	19	20
4	36	89	23	2
76	33	76	99	47
83	19	43	86	80
+ 24	+ 43	+ 87	+ 35	+ 97

8	1	6
3	5	7
4	9	2

A   This is a magic square.
The numbers in each row add up to 15.
The numbers in each column and each diagonal also add up to 15.
15 is the **magic total**.

If the totals are all the same the square is a **magic square**.

Copy this square.

1
10	3	

B   (a) Add 2 to the numbers in square A.
Write your anwers in square B.
(b) What is the total for (i) each row _____?
(ii) each column _____?
(iii) each diagonal _____?

(c) Is B a magic square? _____

What is the magic total? _____

Copy this square. Fill in the missing numbers. Use your calculator if you want to.

2
2	15	16	c
13	8	7	10
9	12 b		6
14 a		4	d

This is another magic square.
Find the magic total by adding the numbers in the first column.
Check by adding the numbers across the second row.
Add the three numbers in the second column.
What is the missing number 'a'?
Find the missing number 'b', 'c', and 'd'.

Write: a = _____, b = _____, c = _____, d = _____
Now check **all** the rows, **all** the columns, and **all** the diagonals.
They should all come to the same number.

You need I cm squared paper.
Each unit is I cm.

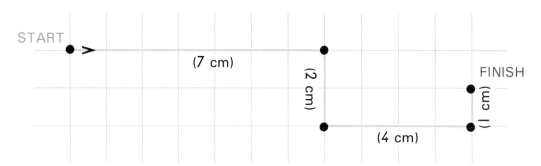

Copy and complete to show the route above.

FORWARD _____. RIGHT 90. FORWARD _____.

LEFT 90. FORWARD _____. LEFT _____. FORWARD _____.

2 Draw these routes on your squared paper.

(a) FORWARD 4. LEFT 90. FORWARD 6.

RIGHT 90. FORWARD 7.

(b) FORWARD 5. RIGHT 90. FORWARD I.
RIGHT 90. FORWARD 8. LEFT 90. FORWARD 2.

3 Write instructions for making (a) the square and (b) the rectangle.

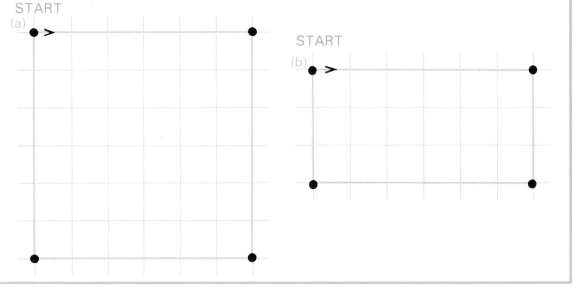

Look at these diagrams:

1 layer

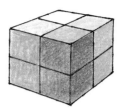

2 layers

There are 4 cubes in each layer.

Get some cubes. Make a layer of four cubes.

How many cubes are there in these layers? Build the layers with cubes if you want to.

Number of layers	1	2	3	4	5	6	7	8	9	10
Number of cubes	4									

Which multiplication table are you making?

Use a calculator to find the number of cubes in (a) 16 layers _____

(b) 23 layers _____   (c) 37 layers _____ .

2

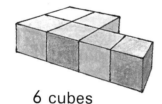

6 cubes

Complete the table below to show the number of cubes for the layers. Use cubes to build the layers if you want to.

Number of layers	1	2	3	4	5	6	7	8	9	10
Number of cubes										

How many cubes did you add on for each extra layer?

Use a calculator to check that the table gives the multiplication table for 6.
Use your calculator to find the number of cubes in:

(a) 14 layers _____   (b) 22 layers _____   (c) 55 layers _____ .

Copy these patterns, and colour the last two shapes to fit the pattern.

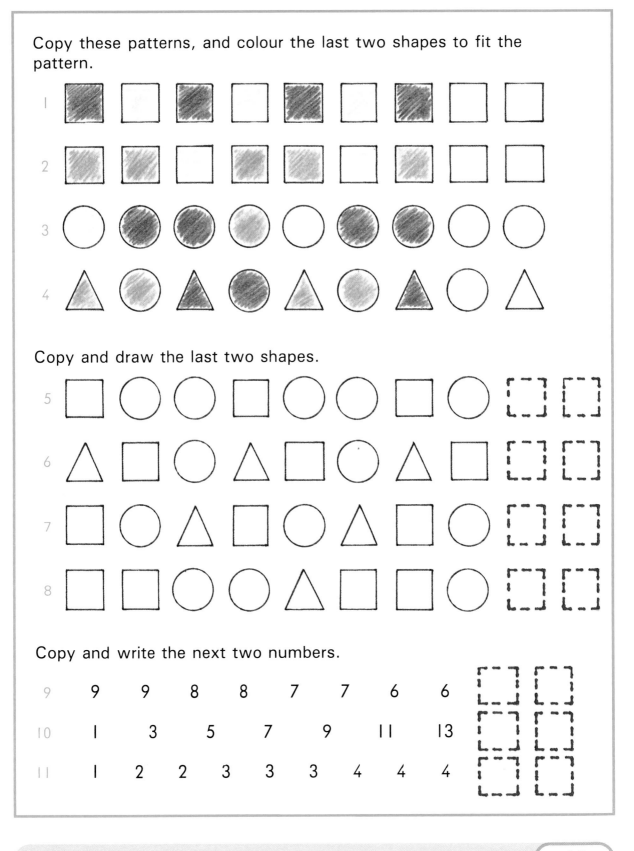

Copy and draw the last two shapes.

Copy and write the next two numbers.

9   9   9   8   8   7   7   6   6

10   1   3   5   7   9   11   13

11   1   2   2   3   3   3   4   4   4

	Likes pears	Does not like pears	
1	Emma	Gino	Likes apples
	Imran	Sarah	Does not like apples

Who likes (a) apples and pears _____

(b) apples, but not pears _____

(c) pears, but not apples _____

(d) who doesn't like apples or pears? _____

	Likes nuts	Does not like nuts	
2			Likes dates
			Does not like dates

Copy this diagram.

Write the names of the children in the correct spaces.

(a) Ashraf likes dates, but does not like nuts.

(b) Ruth likes nuts and dates.

(c) Rob doesn't like dates or nuts.

(d) Tessa likes nuts, but does not like dates.

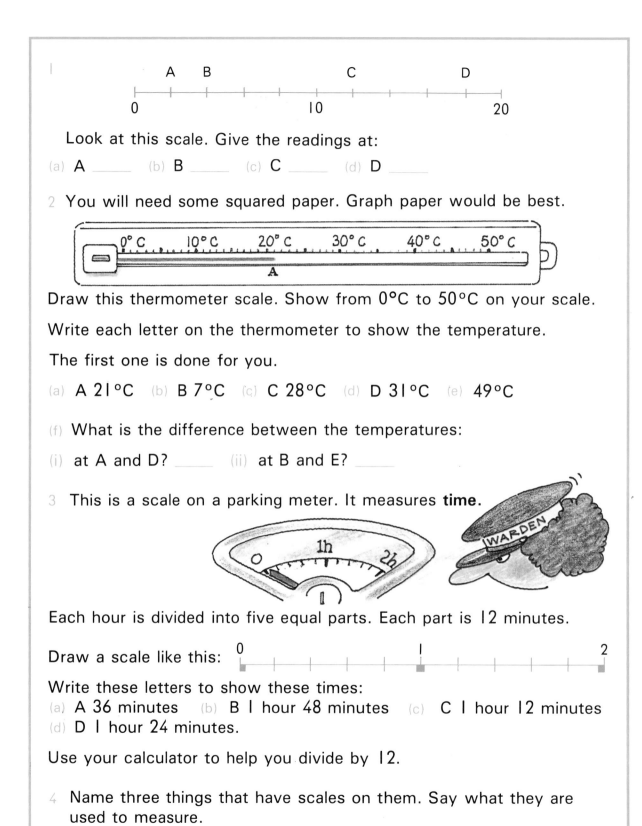

1

	A	B				C		D	
0					10				20

Look at this scale. Give the readings at:

(a) A _____ (b) B _____ (c) C _____ (d) D _____

2 You will need some squared paper. Graph paper would be best.

0°C   10°C   20°C   30°C   40°C   50°C

A

Draw this thermometer scale. Show from 0°C to 50°C on your scale.

Write each letter on the thermometer to show the temperature.

The first one is done for you.

(a) A 21°C   (b) B 7°C   (c) C 28°C   (d) D 31°C   (e) 49°C

(f) What is the difference between the temperatures:

(i) at A and D? _____   (ii) at B and E? _____

3 This is a scale on a parking meter. It measures **time.**

1h   2h

WARDEN

Each hour is divided into five equal parts. Each part is 12 minutes.

Draw a scale like this:

0					1				2

Write these letters to show these times:
(a) A 36 minutes   (b) B 1 hour 48 minutes   (c) C 1 hour 12 minutes
(d) D 1 hour 24 minutes.

Use your calculator to help you divide by 12.

4 Name three things that have scales on them. Say what they are used to measure.

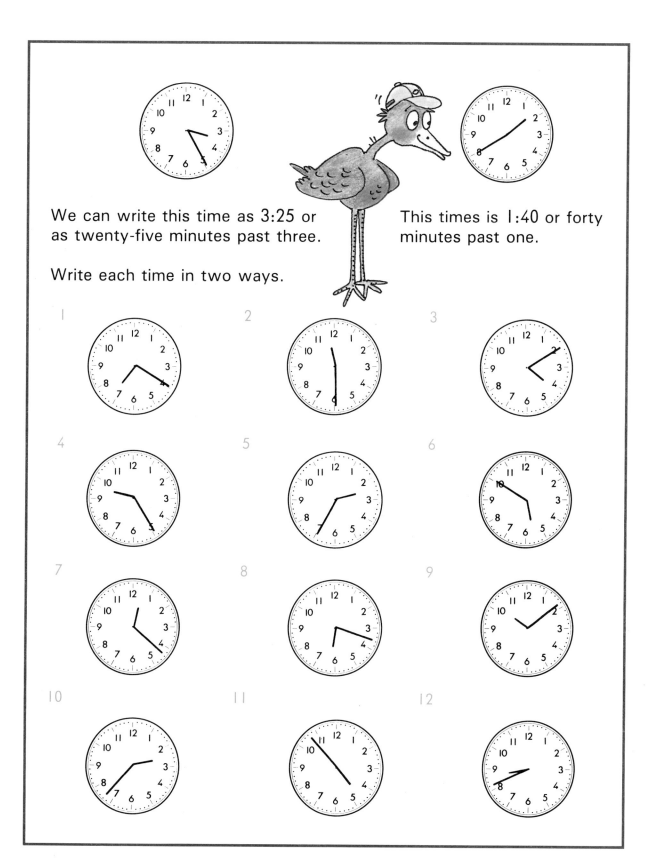

We can write this time as 3:25 or as twenty-five minutes past three.

This times is 1:40 or forty minutes past one.

Write each time in two ways.

Write each time. Then decode the riddle.

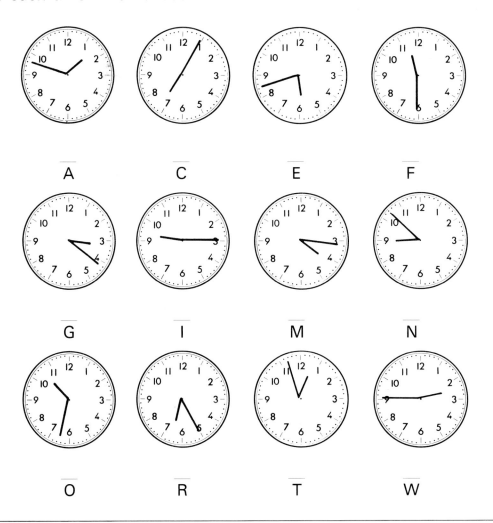

A   C   E   F

G   I   M   N

O   R   T   W

What time is it when an elephant sits on your fence?

12:57   9:15   4:16   5:42   12:57   10:32   3:21   5:42   12:57

___   ___   ___   ___   ___   ___   ___   ___   ___

1:48   8:52   5:42   2:45   11:30   5:42   8:52   7.05   5:42

___   ___   ___   ___   ___   ___   ___   ___   ___

 Steve left school at 3:15 p.m.
He got home at 4:25 p.m.
How long did it take to get home?

He left.				He arrived.
3:15	10 minutes ⟩	3:25	1 hour ⟩	4:25

1 hour and 10 minutes

He left.				He arrived.
3:15	45 minutes ⟩	4:00	25 minutes ⟩	4:25

45 minutes
+ 25 minutes
_____
70 minutes (1 hour and 10 minutes)

How many minutes from:

1 10:45 a.m. to 11:30 a.m.? ___

2 2:22 p.m. to 2:43 p.m.? ___

3 4:15 p.m. to 4:40 p.m.? ___

4 8:05 a.m. to 9.00 a.m.? ___

5 3:38 p.m. to 4:08 p.m? ___

6 6:56 a.m. to 7:31 a.m.? ___

7 9:02 a.m. to 9:47 a.m.? ___

8 12:53 p.m. to 1:53 p.m.? ___

9 7:15 p.m. to 8:40 p.m.? ___

10 11:45 p.m. to 12:50 a.m.? ___

Solve.

11 Cathy left netball practice at 6:50 p.m. She got home at 7:15 p.m. How long did it take her to get home?

12 Roger started his homework at 3:45 p.m. He finished at 4:15 p.m. How long did it take him?

13 Bill wanted to watch a television programme at 8:00 p.m. He turned the television on at 7:35 p.m. How long did he have to wait?

14 The tennis match began at 11:40 a.m. It ended at 1:05 p.m. How long did the match last?

orange	pear	apple	banana
12p	10p	9p	11p

1 Kelly had 30p. How much would she have left if she bought

(a) an orange _____   (b) a pear _____

(c) an apple _____   (d) a banana _____ ?

2 Abel bought an orange and an apple.
He gave the shopkeeper 50p

(a) How much did he spend? _____

(b) How much change did he get? _____

3 Jo bought an orange, a pear and a banana.
She gave the shopkeeper 40p.

(a) How much did she spend? _____

(b) How much change did she get? _____

4 Harry bought 2 oranges.
He was given 26p change.
How much did he give the
shopkeeper?

5 Ruth bought 2 apples.
She was given 2p change.
How much did she give the
shopkeeper?

Your answer to each question will be **add**, **subtract**, **multiply** or **divide**.

1　There are ✦ children in a class.
　　✦ are boys.
　　How many are girls? _____

2　There are ✦ books on each shelf.
　　There are ✦ shelves.
　　How many books? _____

3　There are ✦ sausages in a packet.
　　There are ✦ packets.
　　How many sausages? _____

4　An egg box holds ✦ eggs.
　　There are ✦ eggs.
　　How many egg boxes? _____

5　Each boy had ✦ pence.
　　There are ✦ boys.
　　How many pence? _____

6　A farmer has ✦ black cows and ✦ brown cows.
　　How many cows does he have? _____

7　Ben had ✦ pounds.
　　He spent ✦ pounds.
　　How much money does he have?

8　Each loaf costs ✦ p.
　　Mrs Jones has ✦ p.
　　How many loaves can she buy? _____

9　Jam costs ✦.
　　Beans cost ✦.
　　What is the difference in cost?
　　_____

10　I have ✦ p.
　　Apples cost ✦ p each.
　　How many apples can I buy?
　　_____ .

Solve.

1 There are 6 cars waiting at some traffic lights. Each car has 4 people in it. How many people are there?

2 40 people travelled to a disco in 10 cars. There were the same number of people in each car. How many people were in each car?

3 48 people went to a school football match by car. 36 people walked to the match.
   (a) How many people went to the match altogether?
   (b) How many more went by car than walked?

4 The children at a party ate 30 cakes and 50 biscuits.
   (a) 10 children shared the cakes equally. How many did they have each?
   (b) 5 children shared the biscuits equally. How many did they have each?

5 8 children each drank 2 bottles of cola. How many bottles altogether?

6 8 children each paid 7p for a balloon. What was the total cost?

7 There were 47 boys and 56 girls at a disco.
   (a) How many more girls than boys were there?
   (b) How many children altogether?

The graph shows how many children were at school each day out of a class of 30 children.

Attendance for Class 4A

Monday	🙂🙂🙂🙂🙂🙂🙂🙂
Tuesday	🙂🙂🙂🙂🙂🙂🙂🙂🙂
Wednesday	🙂🙂🙂🙂🙂🙂🙂
Thursday	🙂🙂🙂🙂🙂🙂🙂🙂🙂🙂
Friday	🙂🙂🙂🙂🙂🙂🙂🙂🙂🙂
Each 🙂 shows 3 children.	

1 How many children do these show?

(a) 　(b) 　(c)

2 Draw faces to show:
   (a) 12 children;　(b) 18 children;　(c) 33 children.

3 On which days did all the children come to school?

4 On which day was the greatest number of children absent?

5 How many children came to school on:
   (a) Monday?　(b) Tuesday?　(c) Wednesday?

6 How many more children came on Friday than on Monday?

7 What was the total number of attendances in the week?

(Use your calculator if you want to).

Write the fraction that is coloured.

1

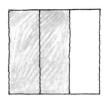

$\dfrac{1}{2}$ $\dfrac{2}{3}$ $\dfrac{2}{4}$

2

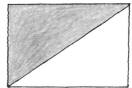

$\dfrac{1}{2}$ $\dfrac{1}{3}$ $\dfrac{1}{4}$

3

$\dfrac{1}{2}$ $\dfrac{1}{4}$ $\dfrac{3}{4}$

4

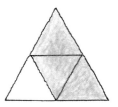

$\dfrac{2}{3}$ $\dfrac{3}{3}$ $\dfrac{3}{4}$

5

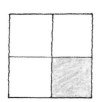

$\dfrac{1}{4}$ $\dfrac{1}{3}$ $\dfrac{1}{2}$

6

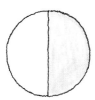

$\dfrac{1}{4}$ $\dfrac{2}{4}$ $\dfrac{3}{4}$

7

$\dfrac{1}{4}$ $\dfrac{2}{4}$ $\dfrac{3}{4}$

8

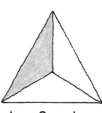

$\dfrac{1}{2}$ $\dfrac{2}{4}$ $\dfrac{1}{3}$

9

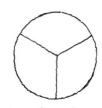

$\dfrac{1}{2}$ $\dfrac{2}{3}$ $\dfrac{2}{4}$

10

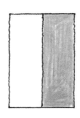

$\dfrac{1}{2}$ $\dfrac{1}{4}$ $\dfrac{1}{3}$

11

$\dfrac{1}{3}$ $\dfrac{2}{3}$ $\dfrac{3}{4}$

12

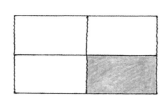

$\dfrac{1}{2}$ $\dfrac{1}{3}$ $\dfrac{1}{4}$

1
(a) What fraction
    is ▢ ?
(b) What fraction
    are ⬭ ?

2
(a) What fraction
    is ⬭ ?
(b) What fraction
    is ▱ ?

3
(a) What fraction
    is ▢ ?
(b) What fraction
    are △ ?

4
(a) What fraction
    are ◇ ?
(b) What fraction
    are ● ?

5
(a) What fraction
    is ⬭ ?
(b) What fraction
    are ▱ ?

6
(a) What fraction
    is ● ?
(b) What fraction
    is ▢ ?

7
(a) What fraction
    is ◇ ?
(b) What fraction
    is ● ?

8
(a) What fraction
    is ▱ ?
(b) What fraction
    are ▢ ?

9
(a) What fraction
    is ◇ ?
(b) What fraction
    are △ ?

INPUT is the number entered into a machine.
OUTPUT is the number that comes out of the machine.

If the INPUT is 6 the OUTPUT is 14.
If the OUTPUT is 20 the INPUT was 12.

1

Add 9	
INPUT	OUTPUT
14	
23	
46	
79	

2

Add 36	
INPUT	OUTPUT
8	
25	
39	
56	

3

Add 44	
INPUT	OUTPUT
9	
18	
37	
49	

4

Subtract 7	
INPUT	OUTPUT
10	
36	
78	
99	

5

Subtract 15	
INPUT	OUTPUT
30	
41	
58	
63	

6

Subtract 29	
INPUT	OUTPUT
42	
67	
83	
92	

7

Add 12	
INPUT	OUTPUT
	38
	46
	51
	73

8

Subtract 20	
INPUT	OUTPUT
	7
	18
	34
	52

9

Subtract 32	
INPUT	OUTPUT
	2
	20
	47
	63

Trace these shapes, and the lines of symmetry.
Draw the missing part to make them symmetrical.

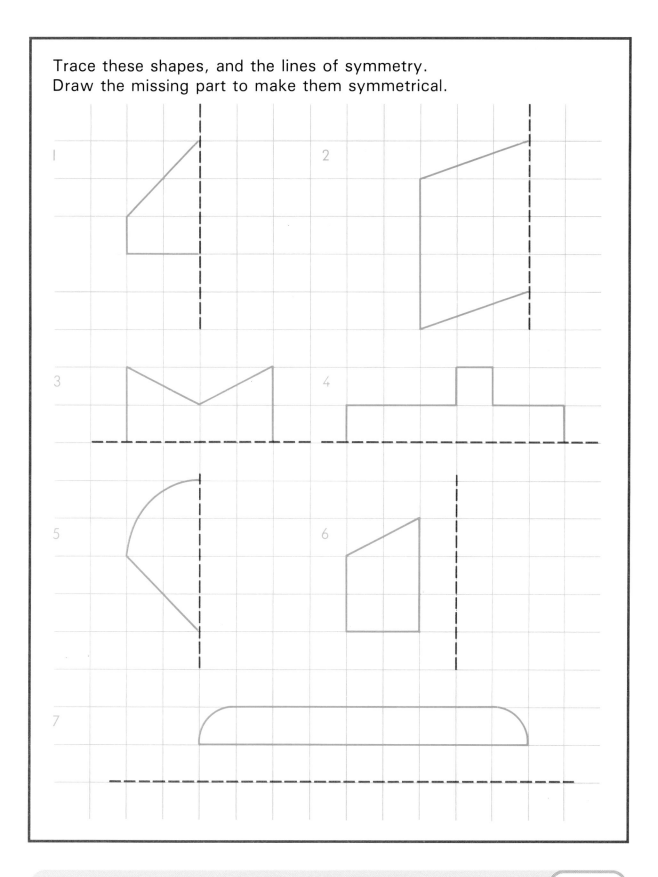

$$4\overline{)35}\ \ ^{8R3}$$
$$-32$$
$$3$$

1 $3\overline{)20}$ 2 $5\overline{)32}$ 3 $4\overline{)25}$

4 $5\overline{)39}$ 5 $5\overline{)41}$ 6 $10\overline{)48}$

7 $3\overline{)25}$ 8 $4\overline{)50}$ 9 $10\overline{)65}$ 10 $3\overline{)10}$

11 $5\overline{)34}$ 12 $2\overline{)19}$ 13 $2\overline{)15}$ 14 $4\overline{)27}$

15 $4\overline{)35}$ 16 $5\overline{)23}$ 17 $3\overline{)11}$ 18 $3\overline{)26}$

19 $10\overline{)71}$ 20 $4\overline{)37}$ 21 $2\overline{)11}$ 22 $3\overline{)19}$

23 $2\overline{)9}$ 24 $10\overline{)58}$ 25 $5\overline{)31}$ 26 $4\overline{)31}$

27 What is the remainder when you divide 19 by:

(a) 2, ___   (b) 3, ___   (c) 4, ___   (d) 5, ___   (e) 10? ___

Use division tests to answer these questions.

You do *not* need to do the divisions.

Check your answers by using a calculator.

1 Write the numbers that **cannot** be divided exactly by 2. (The odd numbers).

11	19	20	38	43	52
100	113	122	158	203	294

2 List all the even numbers that are between 21 and 30.

3 Copy these numbers

15	18	20	35	43	56
65	80	95	100	115	152

Draw a loop round the numbers that can be divided exactly by 5.

Draw a line under the numbers that can be divided exactly by 10.

All the numbers with a line under them also have a loop round them. Can you explain why?

4 Who am I?

(a) I am an even number.
I can be divided exactly by 3.
I am between 13 and 20.

(b) When divided by 5 I have a remainder of 1.
I am an odd number
I am less than 20.

Solve these problems.

1 What is the cost of 4 stamps if each stamp costs:
   (a) 5p?   (b) 7p?   (c) 9p?   (d) 10p?

2 A stamp costs 10p.
   What is the cost of:
   (a) 2 stamps?   (b) 4 stamps?   (c) 6 stamps?   (d) 10 stamps?

3 How much money would you have left if you had:
   (a) 70p and bought four 7p stamps?
   (b) 90p and bought five 9p stamps?
   (c) 80p and bought ten 5p stamps?

4 Find the total cost of:
   (a) three stamps costing 7p each and seven stamps costing 10p each;
   (b) four stamps costing 9p each and six stamps costing 5p each.

5 Find the change from 70p if you buy two stamps costing 8p each and four stamps costing 4p each.

6 A sheet contains 45 stamps costing 8p each.
   There are 5 stamps in each row.
   (a) What is the cost of the stamps in one row?
   (b) How many rows are there?

Copy this number line.

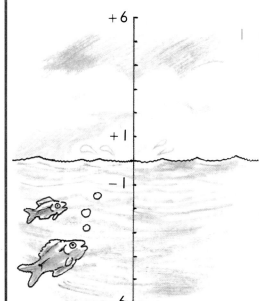

+6
+1
-1
-6

1 (a) Write the missing numbers in the line.
  (b) Write these letters on your line:
      (i)   A at +5   (ii) B at −2
      (iii) C at −5   (iv) D at 0.
  (c) What number will you be at if you go
      (i)   2 up from −4? ___
      (ii) 3 down from +1? ___
      (iii) 4 down from 0? ___

  (d) You start at +1.
      Where will you be if you go down 5
      and then up 2?

2 Copy this temperature scale.
  (It will be easier on squared paper).

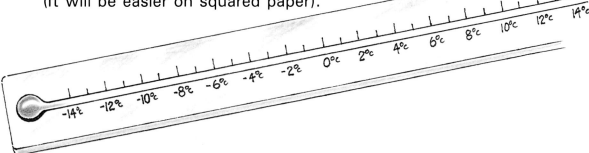

-14°c -12°c -10°c -8°c -6°c -4°c -2°c 0°c 2°c 4°c 6°c 8°c 10°c 12°c 14°c

  (a) Write A where the temperature is 9°C and B where it is −13°C.

  (b) The temperature is 4°C. What will it be if it
      (i)   rises 7°C? ___   (ii) drops 10°C? ___
      (iii) rises 10°C? ___   (iv) drops 4°C? ___

  (c) The temperature is −3°C. What will it be after rising 8°C and
      then dropping 2°C? ___

Measure each line to the nearest centimentre.

Copy and complete this table.

line	length of line
(a)	cm
(b)	cm
(c)	cm
(d)	cm
(e)	cm
(f)	cm
(g)	cm
Total	cm

Remember
1 metre (m) = 100 centimetres (cm)

Copy and complete.

1   100 cm = ___ m   2   4 m = ___ cm

3   500 cm = ___ m   4   9 m = ___ cm

5   1 m 55 cm = ___ cm   6   3 m 10 cm = ___ cm

7   260 cm = 2 m ___ cm   8   485 cm = 4 m ___ cm

9   546 cm = ___ m ___ cm   10 327 cm = ___ m ___ cm

Solve. Write the answers.

11 Sally ran 100 m, walked 60 m, then ran another 95 m. How far did she travel?

12 One metre of ribbon costs 36p. How much does 25 cm of ribbon cost?

13 Pete walked 1550 m to work. On his way home he called at a shop and walked 2260 m. How far out of his way did he walk?

14 A snail moved 55 cm in the morning, 47 cm in the afternoon and 36 cm in the evening. How far did it travel that day?

Remember   1 metre (m) = 100 centimetres (cm)
            1 kilometre (km) = 1000 metres (m).

Copy and complete

1 3 m = _____ cm

2 5 m 80 cm = _____ cm

3 600 cm = _____ m

4 710 cm = _____ m _____ cm

5 2 km = _____ m

6 8 km 400 m = _____ m

7 3000 m = _____ km

8 9420 m = _____ km _____ m

9 The distances below are all in kilometres

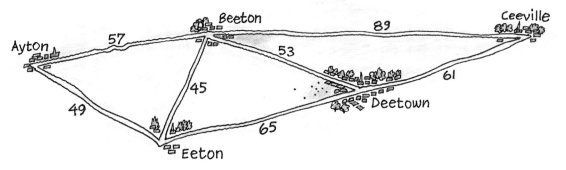

Find the distances:

(a) From Ayton to Beeton and then to Ceeville.

(b) From Deetown to Eeton and back to Deetown.

(c) From Ayton to Ceeville, calling at Eeton and Deetown.

(d) Which is the shortest journey and by how much:

   (i) Beeton to Deetown to Eeton and back to Beeton, or

   (ii) Ayton to Eeton to Beeton and then back to Ayton?

Give each perimeter in centimetres.

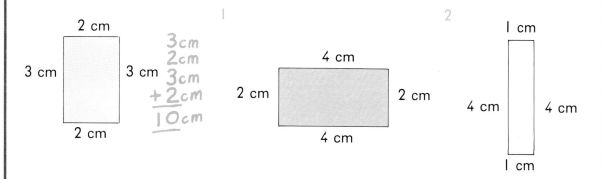

2 cm

3 cm   3 cm

2 cm

3cm
2cm
3cm
+2cm
10cm

1

4 cm

2 cm   2 cm

4 cm

2

1 cm

4 cm   4 cm

1 cm

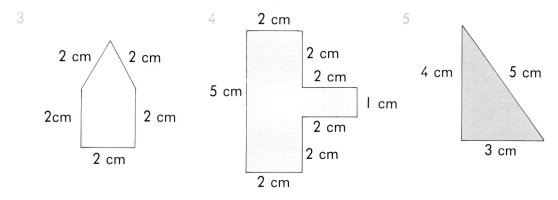

3

2 cm   2 cm

2cm   2 cm

2 cm

4

2 cm

2 cm

2 cm

5 cm   1 cm

2 cm

2 cm

2 cm

5

4 cm   5 cm

3 cm

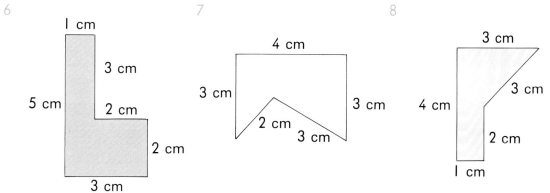

6

1 cm

3 cm

5 cm   2 cm

2 cm

3 cm

7

4 cm

3 cm   3 cm

2 cm

3 cm

8

3 cm

3 cm

4 cm   2 cm

1 cm

9 Copy this table. Complete it by working out the perimeter of each rectangle.

Length in cm	4	3	5	4	5	8
Breadth in cm	2	2	3	1	4	3
Perimeter						

Give the perimeter of each shape.
Then decode to answer the riddle.

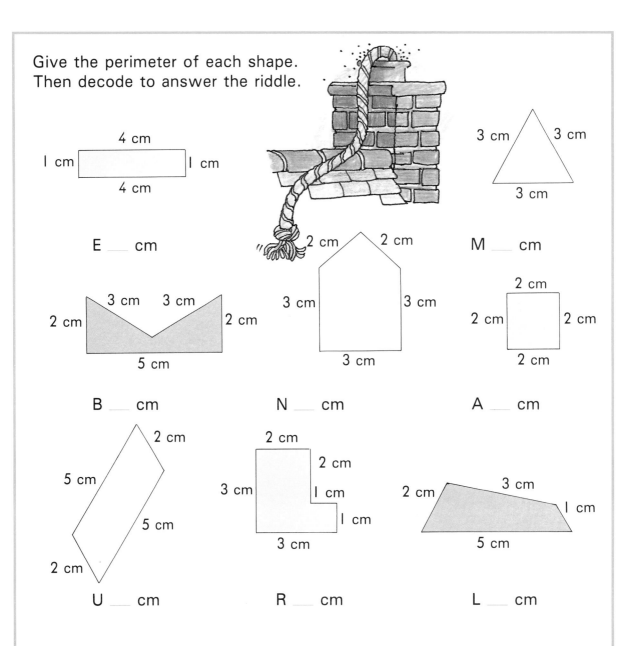

4 cm

I cm   I cm

4 cm

E ___ cm

3 cm   3 cm

3 cm

M ___ cm

3 cm   3 cm

2 cm   2 cm

5 cm

B ___ cm

2 cm   2 cm

3 cm   3 cm

3 cm

N ___ cm

2 cm

2 cm   2 cm

2 cm

A ___ cm

2 cm

5 cm

5 cm

2 cm

U ___ cm

2 cm

2 cm

3 cm   I cm

I cm

3 cm

R ___ cm

2 cm   3 cm

I cm

5 cm

L ___ cm

What can go up a chimney down but can't go down a chimney up?

8 cm 13 cm 14 cm 9 cm 15 cm 12 cm 10 cm 11 cm 11 cm 8 cm

___ ___ ___ ___ ___ ___ ___ ___ ___ ___

Write the unit you would use to measure these things.

For example: Length of a pencil.

feet, centimetres, litres, kilograms, metres.
centimetres

1 Medicine on a spoon.
litres, pints, grams, metres, millilitres.

2 A bag of potatoes.
pounds, grams, metres, pints, litres.

3 Distance travelled by a bus in a day.
kilograms, metres, litres, yards, kilometres.

4 Length of a dress.
kilometres, inches, yards, pints, miles.

5 Distance you could walk in 2 hours.
centimetres, feet, miles, kilograms, millilitres.

6 Weight of a letter.
pounds, grams, feet, kilograms, millilitres.

7 Petrol needed to fill a car's tank.
pints, millilitres, metres, litres, grams.

You need a red bead (R), a blue bead (B) and a yellow bead (Y).
You also need a bag to put the beads in.

I   Put three beads in the bag and shake it.

Draw a table like the one below to enter your results in.
It should go up to 12 (or more if you like).

Number of times		Colour of first bead	Colour of second bead	Colour of third bead
	1			
	2			
	3			
	4			
	5			
	6			

Do this:

Take out one bead. Use Y, R or B to write the colour on your
table in the first column. Take out another bead. Enter the result
in your table in the second column. Take out the third bead. Enter
the colour in the table in the third column.

2 Here are some of the possible results you could have had in
Question 1.
RBY, RYB, YRB, BYR.
(a) How many possible results are there? _____

(b) Make a list of **all** the possible results. _____

3 If you went on with the experiment in Question 1 for a very large
number of times, would each possible result appear the same
number of times? (Write 'Yes' or 'No'.)

1 Write down the days of the week in order. Start with Monday.

2 Write down the months of the year in order.

3 Which is (a) the fifth day of the week?
          (b) the third day of the week?

4 Which is (a) the second month of the year?
          (b) the sixth month of the year?
          (c) the tenth month of the year?

5 Which day of the week is it:
   (a) 3 days after Tuesday?
   (b) 5 days after Friday?
   (c) 2 days before Monday?
   (d) 8 days before Wednesday?

6 What month will it be:
   (a) 3 months after January?
   (b) 6 months after October?
   (c) 4 months before July?
   (d) 5 months before April?

7 Change to days.
   (a) 1 week 4 days   (b) 2 weeks 6 days   (c) 3 weeks 1 day

8 Change 29 days to weeks and days.

This is a report about a farm trip.

The Farm Trip
  Our class visited the Snowden farm. There were
5 children in one car, 4 in another car and 12 in
the mini bus. When we got there, the farmer showed
us around the farm. We saw 8 black cows in one
field and 7 brown cows in another. There were
13 pigs in the pen. 6 of the pigs were white and
the rest of the pigs were brown. The farmer
pointed out that 7 of his ducks were on the pond.
He said he had 12 ducks altogether and that 5 of
them were brown. After being shown around,
we had lunch and went back to school.

Use the information in the story to answer these questions.

(Use your calculator if you want to).

1 How many children came to
   the farm by car?

2 How many children came to
   the farm altogether?

3 How many brown cows did
   they see?

4 How many cows did the
   farmer have in the two fields?

5 How many of the pigs in the
   pen were brown?

6 How many animals were
   brown?

7   (a) How many ducks were on the pond?
    (b) How many ducks were not on the pond?

8   How many cows and pigs did they see altogether?

9   How many animals did they see altogether?

10 It costs £2 a week to feed a pig.
    How much does it cost a week to feed:
    (a) all the white pigs?
    (b) all the brown pigs?

11 One cow gave 9 litres of milk each day.
    How many litres would she give in:
    (a) 3 days?   (b) 6 days?   (c) I week?

12 A duck laid 5 eggs each week.
    How many eggs would it lay in:
    (a) 4 weeks?   (b) 8 weeks?   (c) I0 weeks?

Solve these problems.
Write each answer as a sum and as a sentence.

A book costs £3.
A record costs £5.

(a) How much for both?
(b) How much more than the books does the record cost?

(a) £3 + £5 = £8
The cost of both is £8.
(b) £5 − £3 = £2
The record costs £2 more than the book.

1 10 stamps in a book.
A book costs 60p.
All stamps cost the same amount.

(a) How many stamps in 8 books?
(b) What is the cost of 3 books?
(c) How much does I stamp cost?

2 It takes 26 minutes to mow a lawn. It takes 5 minutes to weed a flower bed. There are 4 flower beds and 2 lawns.

(a) How long does it take to mow both lawns?
(b) How long does it take to weed the 4 flower beds?
(c) How long will it take to mow the 2 lawns and weed all the flower beds?

3 A cake costs 20p.
A biscuit costs 2p.

(a) How many biscuits could be bought with 8p?
(b) What is the cost of 2 cakes.
(c) How much more than a biscuit does a cake cost?
(d) What is the cost of a cake and a biscuit?